# 42 Letter Name Of God

# The Mystical Name Of Manifestation

# Copyright information

Kadmon, Baal

42 Letter Name Of God - The Mystical Name Of Manifestation —1st ed

Printed in the United States of America

Cover image : 67189134 - a hebrew text from an old jewish prayer book - © asafeliasonBook
Cover Design: Baal Kadmon

# Disclaimer

# INTRODUCTION

As I have stated in my other books in the "Sacred Names" series, much importance has been given to the names of God. But not only the names, but the letters in which the names of God are derived. The Name itself would be nothing without the energetic qualities of the letters themselves. The tradition in which this is most evident is in the Jewish mystical body of knowledge called the Kabbalah. The Kabbalistic tradition is multifaceted and contains so much hidden wisdom it is often said that one cannot ascertain even a fraction of the mysteries contained in it in a life time...Even in several lifetimes. The tradition is littered with mystical prayers and methods. Some are practically impenetrable. And those that are not impenetrable are often still too complicated to ascertain without metaphysical training.

In this book, we will be discussing an ancient Jewish prayer, often called the " The Kabbalists Prayer" and the "Genesis Prayer". In Hebrew it is called " Ana Bekoach". This powerful prayer on the surface seems like a standard prayer, nothing particularly remarkable is contained within the verses. To most, it is just another prayer, but to those who look, they will find within the text the 42-letter name of God. This name of God is so powerful that just by reciting it and gazing upon the letters, you can gain immense powers from the divine. Powers that can solve all your problems. I know it sounds too good to be true, but this prayer and the 42-letter name of God within its verses has been proven to be very powerful. If you look it up you will find countless testaments to the power of this name.

In this book, we will discuss how to use the 42-letter name of God. Like my other books, before I get to the meat of the topic, I like to give background material, so you can approach your practice with sufficient knowledge. This book will be no exception. I will be covering prayer, The significance of God's names as well as ancillary, but important information that will help you gain greater understanding.

Let us begin.

# Chapter 1: Prayer

Since we will be dealing specifically with a prayer, I would like to touch upon this topic because I feel it is very important.

Prayer has always been with us. Since the dawn of mankind there has always been some form of prayer. Some using words, some using just actions. If you look at all the ancient cave paintings in Lascaux, in France, you see this need to venerate something greater than oneself. Prayer is universal, even the religions that do not have a theological system also have prayer. Prayer is embedded not only into our DNA, but it is embedded into the universe. Prayer brings peace to those who pray and miracles to those who ask. It is a form of Magick. I am willing to wager that people who say they are atheist also say a little prayer at night. I like to say that atheists are all just closet theists. I still believe that, I just don't think a person can truly be an atheist in such a magickal world. I might be naive to think so, but I am willing to wager that it is true.

The word prayer comes from the Latin word PRECARI which means "to entreat, to beg or to ask earnestly". I guess you could say it is a way to develop a kind of rapport with the energy that is the object of the prayer. As you know, there is no one way to pray, I know most religious practices have certain guidelines, but one can prayer privately and away from these traditions as well. Prayer takes many different forms and should be done in the way you feel most empowered. You can sing a song in prayer, recite a mantra or even stay in silence. There is no right or wrong way.

In every single culture prayer is used in some form or another. In all traditions, a tremendous amount of respect is given to prayer. What you pray could be the difference between abundance and poverty. What you pray can be the difference between health and illness. **Prayers Are Powerful**!

In the Buddhist and Hindu traditions; prayers are used extensively in the form of mantras. In fact, they are the backbone of meditation practice in these traditions. Mantra prayers are chanted thousands upon thousands of times daily by individuals who have become intoxicated by the **bliss** these prayers bring.

In Judaism, Christianity and Islam, prayers are the backbone to it all. Each tradition ritualizes prayer and makes it an absolute requirement. To be devout, YOU MUST pray in these traditions. That's why prayers are always to be scheduled in your day. I for one do not believe there are absolutes in spirituality, nothing is really mandated in my eyes. However, prayer is such a beautiful thing that I can't imagine the human experience without it. Saying a small prayer at night and upon rising brings so much peace. In light of this, the prayer you will learn later can be done audibly or in your mind. Now I'd like to say, we will mostly be focusing on the 42 Letter Name of God, but it is a good idea to say the prayer as well.

In the next chapter, we will discuss the importance of the names of God.

# Chapter 2: What's In A Name?

In all mystical traditions, the spoken and written name is very powerful. Not only the name of God, but of humans as well. Knowing the name of someone or some force can be the difference between abundance and poverty.

As mentioned earlier, In the Jewish Mystical traditions, the backbone of EVERYTHING is the Name of God. Whole books such as the Sepher Yezirah are dedicated to the power of letters and words and how God used them to create the universe. A select group of Mystics use Gods name and the letters of God's name to change events in time and to pierce the very fabric of the universe.

It is said that if anyone could decipher the true name of God, they would have the power to re-set the entire universe back to its primordial state of being. No one knows the true name of God. However, this does not mean we cannot decipher the other names of God through the various spiritual traditions. As mentioned earlier, In this book, we will harness God's name for manifestation. You will know God's 42 lettered name and thus be able to channel the power of that name to change your life from the inside out. This name, as I said earlier, can be found within the text of the prayer "Ana Bekoach". The English translation is not the original language and thus cannot be used to ascertain the 42 names. We will need to glean these names from the Hebrew original of this prayer. **DO NOT FRET, you do not need to know Hebrew in order to harness the 42-lettered name of God.** All you will need is to gaze at the holy and powerful name and that will suffice. I will also transliterate as necessary. But before we delve into the names, let us understand why Hebrew is such an important language for tapping into the power of God.

# Chapter 3: The Power of Hebrew Letters

(The following is excerpted in part from my book THE 72 NAMES OF GOD - THE 72 KEYS OF TRANSFORMATION)

The Hebrew alphabet, unlike most alphabets is multilayered and contains deep spiritual meanings within each letter. In many ways it is similar to the Sanskrit language in that each letter is significant and in and of itself, contains power in the simple utterance of them. Even just looking at them can convey their power. One does not need to understand what they are looking at in order for the power to transmit. When you look at the sky or at water. Do you truly know what they are? Do you know the exact mathematics behind how they work? Sure, you might know that water is H20. Do you truly know how it came about exactly? Some might say they do, but most of us, including myself have no idea how water works or how the sky doesn't just get sucked out into space. Regardless of my ignorance of how they work, both are keeping me alive. You see what I mean? The same goes for the letters and names you will encounter in this book.

The Hebrew Alphabet is comprised of 22 letters with 5 additional letters that are used at the end of words. In the Ancient and mystical text called the Sefer Yezirah (Book Of Creation), the Hebrew letters are the very foundation of all of creation.  Please reference the chart below of the Hebrew letters. The letters are read from right to left.

מ ם ל ך כ י ט ח ז ו ה ד ג ב א

ת ש ר ק צ ץ פ ף ע ס נ ן

For the purposes of this book I will not go into the meanings of each letter, I am just going to give you an overview as to why the Hebrew letters are so important. For our purposes it does not matter what each letter means since we will be using the letters within the context of individual names. These names, create power and meaning that transcend the individual letters they are comprised of.

As I mentioned earlier, the ancient Jewish mystical text called the Sefer Yezirah presented the power of the Hebrew letters.  Not much is known about the Sefer Yezirah but it is said that it was a mystical text revealed to the patriarch Abraham. This means that from the earliest days of humanity, someone knew the secrets to creation. Through the years many mystics of the Jewish faith have studied it. Some have even used the letters to create miracles.

The Hebrew letters come directly from God. Within them contain the secrets of all there is. If one were to decipher their power, one could ascertain the precise roadmap God used to create the universe. In many ways, each and every letter is infused with God's manifestation power.

The Hebrew alphabet looks rather simple when you look at it but that is the beauty of it. Within the letters, the deepest secrets of the cosmos reside.

Each and every single letter is creative in some way, shape or form. They are often expressed as residing in 3 levels.

Letters 1-9: Reside in the primordial or archetypal level.

Letters 10-18: Reside in the world or level of creation and manifestation.

Letters 19-22: Resides in the supernal or cosmic level.

When you simply gaze at them you are activating creative worlds. It is for this reason we will be using the 42-lettered name of God in their original Hebrew font. Since the letters together create the energy force within the name.

As you can see, this was a brief overview as to why the Hebrew letters are so powerful. I could have gone on for several hundred pages about each one, but I figure you bought this book to gain access to this power now.  If you would like to learn more about the Hebrew letters and their significance, there is a great book called "The Wisdom In the Hebrew Alphabet".

Let us know discuss the 42 Lettered Name of God and where it comes from.

# Chapter 4: The 42 Letter Name Of God

If you have read the other books in this series, you will know that I have covered extensively the hidden names of God. Often, they are hidden within a particular set of verses. The 42 letter Name of God is no exception. Like the 72 names of God I discuss in previous books, the name is embedded into a set of verses. Unlike the 72 names of God however, the 42-letter name is derived from the verses of a particular prayer. Whereas the 72 names of God were derived from the book of Exodus. If you would to learn more about that please go to (THE 72 NAMES OF GOD - THE 72 KEYS OF TRANSFORMATION)

The prayer in question is called "Ana Bekoach".

This prayer was written around the 1 or 2 century A.D. by a mystical rabbi named Rabbi Nehonia. The prayer is composed of 7 lines that contain 6 words in each line. Each line bestows certain powers. Within each line contains several letters that, together, create the 42 names of God. The first letter of each word in the prayer together, composes the name of God. (I will illustrate this shortly). This prayer is of utmost importance because within that name, the powers of all of creation is present. Like the Hidden name in Genesis, I discussed in a previous book, this name too helps you tap into the very power of creation and manifestation.

Here is the prayer in Hebrew. I will highlight in yellow the letters that compromise the name of God.

אָנָּא בְּכֹחַ גְּדֻלַּת יְמִינְךָ תַּתִּיר צְרוּרָה׃
קַבֵּל רִנַּת עַמְּךָ שַׂגְּבֵנוּ טַהֲרֵנוּ נוֹרָא
נָא גִבּוֹר דּוֹרְשֵׁי יִחוּדְךָ כְּבָבַת שָׁמְרֵם
בָּרְכֵם טַהֲרֵם רַחֲמֵי צִדְקָתְךָ תָּמִיד גָּמְלֵם
חֲסִין קָדוֹשׁ בְּרוֹב טוּבְךָ נַהֵל עֲדָתֶךָ
יָחִיד גֵּאֶה לְעַמְּךָ פְּנֵה זוֹכְרֵי קְדֻשָּׁתֶךָ
שַׁוְעָתֵנוּ קַבֵּל וּשְׁמַע צַעֲקָתֵנוּ יוֹדֵעַ תַּעֲלוּמוֹת

I will extract the letters to reveal the full name:

אב"ג ית"ץ

קר"ע שט"ן

נג"ד יכ"ש

בט"ר צת"ג

חק"ב טנ"ע

יג"ל פז"ק

שק"ו צי"ת

Below I will transliterate the prayer from the Hebrew as well as provide a translation:

**Ana bekoach, gedulat yemincha, tatir tzrura**

**Kabel rinat amcha sagveinu, ta-ha-reinu nora**

**Na gibor dorshey yichudcha, kvavat shamrem**

**Barchem taharem, rachamei tzidkatcha**

Tamid gamlem, chasin kadosh

Berov tuvcha, nahel adatecha

Yachid geeh leamcha pney, zochrei kdushatecha

Shavateinu kabel ushma tzaakateinu, yodea taalumot

Translation:

We beg you with the strength and greatness of your right arm. Accept your people's song, elevate and purify us. Please, Oh heroic one, those who pursue your unique qualities - guard them as the pupil of an eye. Bless them, purify them and pity them, may your righteousness always reward them.

Powerful and most Holy One, in goodness guide your flock. Oh you Unique and proud one, to your people turn, who remember your holiness. Accept our cries, and hear our scream, oh knower of mysteries. Now we will go over how to pronounce each of the names from the Hebrew.

As I mentioned earlier, each line in the Hebrew represents a power of manifestation. I will elucidate each line for your reference.

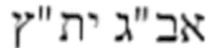

אב"ג ית"ץ

ABAG EE-TATZ

קְרַ"ע שְׂטַ"ן

**KA-RAH SAW-TAN**

נְגַ"ד יְכַ"שׁ

**NAH-GAD EE-CHASH**

בְּטַ"ר צְתַ"ג

**BAH-TAR TZA-TAG**

חֲקַ"ב טְנַ"ע

**CHA-KAV TAH-NAH**

יְגַ"ל פְּזַ"ק

**EE-GAL PAH-ZAK**

שְׁקַ"ו צְיַ"ת

# SHAH-KAV TZAH-YAT

As I mentioned earlier, each line represents a different manifestation power. I will elucidate upon them below.

**Line 1**: This line is the most powerful of the prayer. The 6 letters on this line that comprise part of the name of God is considered very protective. If you are in dire need, no matter what need, you can focus on this name and God will come to your aid. We will do a protection ritual later in this book using this name. You can use it for other needs as well. I will just use protection as an example.

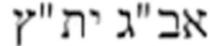

**ABAG EE-TATZ**

**Line 2**: This line bestows supernatural abilities to control events around you and to control negative entities as well. Negative entities can be either spiritual or human for that matter. We will perform a ritual to change an outcome of an event or to push an event to conform to your desired outcome.

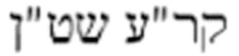

KA-RAH SAW-TAN

**Line 3**: If you have a difficult decision to make or are lost as to what way to take in your life, this aspect of the name will help you. We will perform a ritual that will help you gain clarify on a decision.

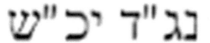

NAH-GAD EE-CHASH

**Line 4**: This will help you gain the strength to preserver on anything you need. It will help you achieve your goals. We will do a ritual on goal attainment later in this book.

BAH-TAR TZA-TAG

**Line 5**: This aspect of the name will grant you psychic powers, especially the ability to tell the future. We will perform a ritual on developing intuition and psychic powers.

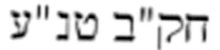

CHA-KAV TAH-NAH

**Line 6**: This aspect of the name will bestow inner peace and tranquillity as well as spiritual insights into any problem you might have. We will perform a ritual to gain insight and understanding on an issue that has been plaguing you.

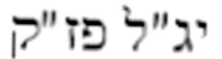

EE-GAL PAH-ZAK

**Line 7**: If you need to reset your life and start fresh, this aspect of the name will do this for you. We will perform a ritual to get a new start in your life in the following chapter.

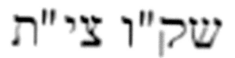

**SHAH-KAV TZAH-YAT**

As you can see, this 42-letter name is very powerful and can help you in pretty much all aspects of your life.

# Chapter 5: Using The 42 Letter Name of God

In this chapter we will begin to use the power of the 42 letter Name of God. Each page contains one ritual. The Instruction are simple.

Gaze at the letters as you visualize the outcome you want. Pronounce the letters once. Let the letters permeate your entire vision. Let the letters hold your thoughts as you visualize the outcome you want. By doing this you are tapping directly into the power of the name. Once the energy feels suffused in you, you may end the ritual.

It's as simple as that. No need to make something so powerful so complicated. Do this as often as you like. I do have a feeling that once you do it once or twice, you will FEEL that change is coming.

Now, let's get started, lets tap into the awesome power of the 42 Letter Name Of God.

# 1: Protection

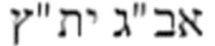

ABAG EE-TATZ

**Ritual:**

**Please take a moment and relax.**

**While looking at the letters, think about your need for protection.**

**Pronounce ABAG EE-TATZ**

**Now imagine the letters pulsating with energy around you and protecting you.**

**Once you feel that it has worked. You can stop the ritual. Do this as often as you like.**

# 2: Change an Event

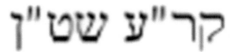

KA-RAH SAW-TAN

**Ritual:**

**Please take a moment and relax.**

**While looking at the letters, think about an event you would like to change in your favor or to gain the desired outcome you want.**

**Pronounce KA-RAH SAW-TAN**

**Now imagine the letters pulsating with energy. Visualize the event and how you want it to unfold. Imagine the letters surrounding the objects or people involved in this event.**

**Once you feel that it has worked. You can stop the ritual. Do this as often as you like.**

# 3: To Gain Insight

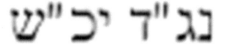

NAH-GAD EE-CHASH

### Ritual:

Please take a moment and relax.

While looking at the letters, think about the issue you need to gain clarity on.

Pronounce NAH-GAD EE-CHASH

Now imagine the letters pulsating with energy around you. Visualize the situation you need clarity on. Sit with this as long as you wish

Once you feel that it has worked. You can stop the ritual. Do this as often as you like.

# 4: To Attain Your Goals

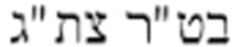

BAH-TAR TZA-TAG

**Ritual:**

Please take a moment and relax.

While looking at the letters, think about the goal you want to achieve.

Pronounce BAH-TAR TZA-TAG

Now imagine the letters pulsating with energy around you. Visualize the goal and the desired outcome.

Once you feel that it has worked. You can stop the ritual. Do this as often as you like. PLEASE DO THIS RIGHT BEFORE YOU ARE PERFORMING AN ACTIVITY RELATED TO YOUR ULTIMATE GOAL. IT WILL GIVE YOU MOTIVATION.

# 5: To Attain Psychic Powers

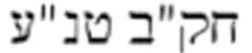

חק"ב טנ"ע

CHA-KAV TAH-NAH

## Ritual:

Please take a moment and relax.

While looking at the letters, think about your desire for psychic powers OR for insight into the future regarding anything you desire.

**Pronounce** CHA-KAV TAH-NAH

Now imagine the letters pulsating with energy around you. Sit and think about your need for psychic power. See what flashes in your mind.

Once you feel that it has worked. You can stop the ritual. Do this as often as you like. It is a good idea to have a recorder nearby or a pad and pen to record/write the psychic messages you get from this ritual.

# 6: To Attain Inner Peace And Tranquility On An Issue

יג"ל פז"ק

EE-GAL PAH-ZAK

## Ritual:

Please take a moment and relax.

While looking at the letters, think about your need for inner peace and tranquility regarding an event or a situation.

Pronounce EE-GAL PAH-ZAK

Now imagine the letters pulsating with energy around you. Sit and think about this issue and let the letters surround you and enter you as they bring you peace.

Once you feel that it has worked. You can stop the ritual. Do this as often as you like.

# 7: To Have A Fresh start - Reset Your Life.

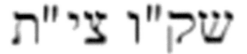

שַׁקָ"וּ צִי"ת

SHAH-KAV TZAH-YAT

## Ritual:

Please take a moment and relax.

While looking at the letters, think about your need for a fresh start and a reset on your life or a situation.

**Pronounce** SHAH-KAV TZAH-YAT

Now imagine the letters pulsating with energy around you. Sit and think about resetting your life and allow yourself to give up any feelings of guilt. We all desire a second chance and a clean slate when life gets out of control.

Once you feel that it has worked. You can stop the ritual. Do this as often as you like. I suggest doing this in the morning time upon awaking.

# Conclusion

We have come to the end of this text. I know it might not seem like much, but what you have just learned here will unlock your potential in ways that other texts cannot do. Often, we are beguiled by overly complex methods of transformation. We think " if it is elaborate and complex, it must be good." This, my friend, is not the case. Our connection with spirit is meant to be easy, not hard. Anyone who tells you that we must work and toil in order to connect to God is not telling you the truth. Just on a logical basis alone it doesn't make sense to have to toil to BE what you already ARE. All it takes is some mindfulness and knowing. I am not saying that transformation doesn't require inner work, it does. But the methods to get there do not and are not meant to be complicated.
**Less is More.**

I am confident that by simply gazing at the letters of the 42-lettered name you will gain great benefit.

Thank you,

Baal Kadmon

# Occult Courses

Over the years, I have received many hundreds of emails asking me if I would ever consider creating online video courses. At first, I was unsure. After so many emails, I decided it was time.

**I am now offering courses.**

If it interests you in learning more about the **Occult, Meditation, Ancient Languages and History**, you will not be disappointed.

**All courses will all be accessible, informative and affordable.**

Please go to www.occultcourses.com

There you will find my current courses and all the upcoming courses. If you see a current course you are interested in, you can sign up and get **instant access.**

If you see a future course that interests you, sign up to the mailing list and I will notify you upon its release.

All courses come with a **30-day, no questions asked, money-back guarantee**. If a course is not for you, just let me know, and I will refund you.

Please go to www.occultcourses.com

# Want to Enhance Your Rituals?

I am not one to promote myself. I like to keep things low-key, but I created a new service that has proven to enhance your rituals and your state of mind and I am very excited about it. As many of you may know, I use Brainwave Entrainment Audios to enhance my writing, my rituals and a lot more. I have been using brainwave products since the 80s. I am using one now as I write this.

I have created hyper-specific Brainwave audios geared to specific spiritual entities. For example, if you call upon the demon, King Paimon, I have a specific audio for him. If you work with the Hindus Goddess Lakshmi, I have a Brainwave Audio for her as well.

Please visit: www.occultmindscapes.com

I am adding Audios every week and will have something for everyone and for every tradition. I am only charging $3.95 per audio MP3 download, with steep discounts for multiple purchases.

I think you will LOVE them. My beta testers loved them, and I am confident you will find them useful as well.

# Other Books By The Author

**Organized by date of publication from most recent:**

Shiva Mantra Magick: Harnessing The Primordial

Tefillin Magick: Using Tefillin For Magickal Purposes (Jewish Magick Book 1)

Jesus Magick (Bible Magick Book 2)

The Magickal Moment Of Now: The Inner Mind of the Advanced Magician

The Magick Of Lilith: Calling Upon The Great Goddess of The Left Hand Path (Mesopotamian Magick Book 1)

The Magickal Talismans of King Solomon

Mahavidya Mantra Magick: Tap Into the 10 Goddesses of Power

Jinn Magick: How to Bind the Jinn to do Your Bidding

Magick And The Bible: Is Magick Compatible With The Bible? (Bible Magick Book 1)

The Magickal Rites of Prosperity: Using Different Methods To Magickally Manifest Wealth

Lakshmi Mantra Magick: Tap Into The Goddess Lakshmi for Wealth and Abundance In All Areas of Life

Tarot Magick: Harness the Magickal Power of the Tarot

The Quantum Magician: Enhancing Your Magick With A Parallel Life

Tibetan Mantra Magick: Tap Into The Power Of Tibetan Mantras

The 42 Letter Name of God: The Mystical Name Of Manifestation (Sacred Names Book 6)

Tara Mantra Magick: How To Use The Power Of The Goddess Tara

Vedic Magick: Using Ancient Vedic Spells To Attain Wealth

The Daemonic Companion: Creating Daemonic Entities To Do Your Will

Tap Into The Power Of The Chant: Attaining Supernatural Abilities Using Mantras (Supernatural Attainments Series

72 Demons Of The Name: Calling Upon The Great Demons Of The Name (Sacred Names Book 5)

Moldavite Magick: Tap Into The Stone Of Transformation Using Mantras (Crystal Mantra Magick Book 1)

Ouija Board Magick - Archangels Edition: Communicate And Harness The Power Of The Great Archangels

Chakra Mantra Magick: Tap Into The Magick Of Your Chakras (Mantra Magick Series Book 4)

Seed Mantra Magick: Master The Primordial Sounds Of The Universe (Mantra Magick Series Book 3)

The Magick Of Saint Expedite: Tap Into The Truly Miraculous Power Of Saint Expedite (Magick Of The Saints Book 2)

Kali Mantra Magick: Summoning The Dark Powers of Kali Ma (Mantra Magick Series Book 2)

Mary Magick: Calling Forth The Divine Mother For Help (Magick Of The Saints Book 1)

# About Baal Kadmon

Baal Kadmon is an Author, and Occultist based out of New York City. In addition to the Occult, he is a Scholar of Religious, Philosopher and a Historian specializing in Ancient History, Late Antiquity and Medieval History. He has studied and speaks Israeli Hebrew · Classical Hebrew · Ugaritic language · Arabic · Judeo-Aramaic · Syriac (language) · Ancient Greek and Classical Latin.

Baal first discovered his occult calling when he was very young. It was only in his teens, when on a trip to the Middle East that he heeded the call. Several teachers and many decades later he felt ready to share what he has learned.

His teachings are unconventional to say the least. He includes in-depth history in almost all the books he writes, in addition to rituals. He shatters the beloved and idolatrously held notions most occultists hold dear. His pared-down approach to Magick is refreshing and is very much needed in a field that is mired by self-important magicians who place more importance on pomp and circumstance rather than on Magick. What you learn from Baal is straight forward, with no frills. Magick is about bringing about change or a desired result; Magick is a natural birthright...There is no need to complicate it.

Follow Him on Facebook and other Social Media Sites:
**http://baalkadmon.com/social-media/**

# CLASS 10'S
# CHANCE TO SHINE

*To the staff and pupils at*
*Bentley Heath C of E Primary School,*
*past and present, for all the happiness they*
*have brought to my children. RW*


*To my husband, James,*
*with thanks for all his support. VH*